The
Railway Vanishes

At Cricklewood shed, 1963.

The
Railway Vanishes

An appreciation of a lost era

H. G. Forsythe ARPS

Silver Link Publishing Ltd

Top Shed, King's Cross, 1958: Passed Fireman Jack Walsh on the footplate of 'A3' 'Pacific' No 60103 *Flying Scotsman*.

© H. G. Forsythe, 1992

First published in November 1992
Reprinted March 1993
Reprinted June 1993

British Library Cataloguing in Publication Data

Forsythe, H. G.
    Railway Vanishes: Appreciation of a Lost Era
    I. Title
    385.0941

ISBN 0 947971 95 5

Silver Link Publishing Ltd
Unit 5
Home Farm Close
Church Street
Wadenhoe
Peterborough PE8 5TE
Tel/fax (08015) 4-4-0

Printed and bound in Great Britain

Contents

Acknowledgements

The author would like to thank most warmly Mr Jack Gardner for invaluable background information without which it would not have been possible to compile this book. Jack Gardner, who has retired from British Rail, is currently Steam Inspector at the Great Western Society Depot at Didcot and Diesel Inspector of the Severn Valley Railway. He is author of the definitive book *Castles to Warships* published by John Murray which gives a unique insight into the changeover from steam to diesel traction from the railwayman's point of view. Thanks also to Alan Eaton for valuable timetable information and, of course, to all the railwaymen who in the past so kindly allowed me to photograph so many of their activities. Special thanks are due to my wife who, in years gone by, cheerfully put up with blistered feet on hot and grimy platforms while forced to hang around London stations waiting for me to get that ever-elusive perfect picture, and particularly for her help in choosing photographs and correcting the manuscript. Acknowledgement must also be made to the excellent series of booklets *What Happened to Steam* published by Peter Hands; these slim volumes are an absolute must for anyone interested in the last days of steam in Great Britain.

All photographs, unless otherwise acknowledged, were taken by the author using a Leica IIIf camera fitted with either an Elmar f/3.5 50 mm lens or an Elmar f/3.5 35 mm lens. A few pictures, notably of *Flying Scotsman* at Top Shed, were taken using a Rolleiflex Twin Lens Reflex. The in-cab action pictures were taken with the Leica at a shutter speed of 1/500 sec using bulb flash as fill-in illumination.

That unmistakeable Great Western look - 'Castle' Class No 5000 *Launceston Castle* at Swindon Shed in 1961. No 5000 was looking very smart after her final overhaul, but she was withdrawn in November 1964 and was scrapped at Birds, Morriston, Swansea, in April 1965.

Introduction

Progress is the name of the game. Anyone yearning for the 'good old days' is immediately labelled a hopelessly unrealistic nostalgic sentimentalist with his head well and truly buried in the sand - and yet - and yet . . .

The old railway we knew and loved has vanished. Steam is dead, replaced by diesels who themselves are being replaced by electrics. Old landmarks have gone; the magnificent crossing at Newcastle, for instance, has disappeared. York Station has lost its centre roads, and so has Bournemouth. Both are now reminiscent of some broken down Third World edifice - decaying monuments to colonial builders of the past.

Speed is the spur. Nowadays we can rush between cities at 125 to 150 miles per hour. The journey between London and Edinburgh on today's 'Flying Scotsman' takes only 4 hr 8 min with three stops *en route*. Maybe that is just as well as you may be expected to stand all the way. The steam-hauled 'Flying Scotsman' took just over 8 hours with no stops at all, but you were certain of a seat and you got 1st Class service throughout the train and the journey.

In those days the journey may have been slow but what a delight it was. When you turned up at King's Cross the coaches were already in the station and you could get on board at your leisure without having to queue in a drafty concourse while a hasty 'lick and a promise' is given to the just arrived HST or electric set by reluctant station cleaners.

You would be shown to your reserved seat by courteous station staff and a porter would carry your baggage. No problem with some yob who has occupied your reserved seat and belligerently refuses all (timid) efforts of train staff to dislodge it, him or her. You would be in a compartment coach and there is plenty of room at your seat. No table strategically placed so that when you stand up painful pressure is applied to your legs - presumable to make you sit down again sharpish. No blaring sound system which might mean violence for you if you ask for it to be turned down.

Meals and refreshments were available all through your journey. No closing down 'for cashing up' after Newcastle or sooner. Today on the Western Region, in the up direction, they are often closed before Reading.

In the then fairly rare event of a substantial delay, train staff would inform passengers of the problem. If restaurant cars were on the train, passengers would be served as long as supplies held out. Not like a recent case when, during a hold-up of several hours not far from Welwyn Garden City, staff resolutely refused to open up the Buffet. In those days toilets were clean and actually had water in them. But to hanker after those times is probably unrealistic and certainly hor-

The romance of the railway. A passing cyclist savours the unforgettable spectacle of a steam-hauled down express in full flight at Langley on the East Coast Main Line on a summer Saturday in 1960.

ribly nostalgic. However, let's look for a moment at more mundane matters - like being a commuter in and out of central London.

In the early 'fifties I lived in Ealing, later at Raynes Park, and I worked in London WC1. I used to catch a Western Region suburban train from Ealing Broadway which got me in to the far end of Paddington Station - Paddington Suburban - within 10 minutes or so. All I had to do was cross over the platform and pick up a Metropolitan line train to Euston Square. I do not remember delays of any kind ever holding me up to and from work. On the Southern Region I remember no real troubles. On foggy nights a 'Fog Service' operated with a modified timetable, but you still got home without undue delay. Signal failures were rare and when they did happen disruption was highly localised. It is true that points froze up in very cold weather, but extended and regular delays due to 'the wrong kind of snow' or too many autumn leaves were quite unheard of. Progress has brought these new problems to plague us.

Trains in those days were reliable. Now, commuters on certain lines never know whether they will get to work or home on time - or at all. During the last war the Luftwaffe's bombs caused relatively minor disruption of rail services. A bomb would knock out a station sometimes, but services were back to normal in short order. With the new centralised and computerised signalling system, a small fire in a junction box is all that is needed to disrupt service at several London stations for days. The old fail-safe mechanisms of mechanical signalling did not always prevent accidents, but they certainly would not have allowed an accident like that at Clapham to occur. Computerised re-signalling of the Severn Tunnel led directly to the very first collision in that famous Great Western link. Continuing poor service on certain commuter lines has been officially ascribed by British Rail to the fact that 'two computers were unable to speak to each other'! Such, dear reader, is the stuff that progress is made of and which we are told we are hopelessly cranky if we criticise.

Steam, of course, simply had to go. After all, steam locomotives were dirty, polluting, labour intensive and cost more to operate than the new diesel motive power.

Hundreds of thousands of words have been written about the Modernisation Programme, the Beeching Cuts, the pros and cons of dieselisation of one area at a time, the definite cons of mixing diesel and steam traction together, the lack of proper testing of all the various manufacturers' designs. I do not propose to add many more words to these controversies.

However, it is worth reflecting, 25 years on, on a few significant points.

Steam was *not* the bogey it was made out to be. Much of the dirt and unpleasantness associated with steam locomotion could have been eliminated using modern techniques. Advanced technology could have transformed the efficiency of the steam locomotive as research in South Africa, the old Soviet

Portent of the future. In this 1959 picture the prototype 'Deltic' diesel-electric locomotive stands in the background at King's Cross waiting to follow its coaches out of the platform. In the foreground is 'A4' 'Pacific' No 60022 *Mallard*, having just arrived with an up express. Both locomotives were unique. *Mallard* was, indeed is, the fastest steam locomotive of all time, having reached 126 mph with a test train on 7 July 1938. Owned by the National Railway Museum at York, she ventures out on the main line from time to time. The 'Deltic' was owned by the English Electric Company and ran on test on various parts of BR, notably the Midland and Eastern Regions. It never carried a running number and is now on show at the Science Museum, London. *Photo courtesy of British Railways and taken by G. H. Mapleston of the now defunct Eastern Region Magazine*

Above The summer of 1960 and 'A3' 'Pacific' No 60059 *Tracery* brings an express from the north out of Gasworks Tunnel into the old familiar King's Cross Station. *Tracery* was fitted with a double chimney in 1958 but did not get her German-style smoke deflectors until 1961, only a year before withdrawal and two years before she was scrapped at Doncaster.

Right A very different King's Cross of the 'eighties with revised track layout, overhead electric wires and no familiar signal boxes. An HST approaches.

Union and in the USA has amply demonstrated. At one time, during the OPEC petroleum crisis, it was on the cards that a revolutionary new steamer would emerge in the US. But oil prices slumped and these projects were put on hold. Oil, though, is not an infinite resource and the time *will* come when it will no longer be possible to operate internal combustion engines *in their present form*.

Electric traction is one solution, but there are many lines, indeed many railways, which it simply would not make economic sense to electrify. It will certainly be interesting too to see what happens to gas-guzzling jet aircraft when that time comes - perhaps we will see a return to steam on the railways and airships in the sky.

The steam locomotive is mechanically simple. It could relatively easily be maintained and repaired and did not require high-technology skills and equipment to keep it working. An ideal machine, one would have thought, for use in Third World countries where engineering skills and equipment are not in over-abundant supply. But no - oh dear, no! The railways of the Third World are littered with the corpses of defunct diesels, especially GM diesels - compulsory purchases in exchange for US aid. In the Sudan their diesels all failed and the railway was unable to move desperately needed foodstuffs to famine-hit areas. A British firm was called in to revive some of the steam fleet; motive power that the local railway staff *could* maintain and operate. In view of this experience, it may, to some (naive) people, appear a little surprising that the railways of Zimbabwe have just been instructed by the 'experts' of the World Bank that they must scrap all their steam locomotives and dieselise in return for a loan.

In Turkey they were not even allowed to store their steam engines - they *had* to be scrapped. Is there a vendetta against the steam locomotive? It rather looks like it, doesn't it?

Of course, as every sane and sensible person knows, there has long been a vendetta against the railways headed by the oil and road transport lobbies aided by partisan governments. The railways themselves, plagued by rotten management and short-sighted and ruthless unions, have not helped themselves either. What is really needed is an integrated transport policy making full use of the aspects of rail and road travel which are best suited to the national interest. When you look at the endless streams of heavy lorries moving goods on any motorway - the M25 for example - a naive person may well ask what on earth is the sense of shifting all those goods by road when the railway could do it so much better. Anyone reading this book who has a serious concern for such things and who would like to see a rebirth of the railway and a reversal of the insane policies of killing off trains, would do well to read the excellent book *The Great Railway Conspiracy* by David Henshaw, published in 1991 by Leading Edge.

Today's railways are in some ways a technological marvel, in others a disaster. Few would deny that the last person, these days, to be considered is the unfortunate passenger (now quaintly referred to as a 'customer'). Once railway operations were flexible. Additional demand could easily be met by the simple process of adding some extra coaches to a scheduled express. This cannot easily be done with the multiple unit sets which are now the norm. So 'customers' are expected, at busy times, to stand over very long distances; standing from Newcastle to King's Cross is quite common.

In steam days standby locomotives were always on duty at major stations and even in quite small centres. A breakdown could be dealt with quickly and easily. Today a breakdown means delays of hours while desperate attempts are made to move in a locomotive or set from many miles away. This has even happened to the Royal Train.

Once it was very different. We had a good railway. Not ideal, but at least reasonable. A railway where railwaymen took pride in their job. That railway has now virtually disappeared. What more damning indictment could there possible be of today's railway than a railwayman whose father, grandfather and great grandfather before him had all worked on the railway, saying that the very last place he would like his own son to work is the railway?

In the following pages we will have a look at aspects of the railway of the not too distant past, a railway which has now all but vanished. In *Man and Superman*, George Bernard Shaw wrote:

'The reasonable man adapts himself to the world: the unreasonable one persists in trying to adapt the world to himself. Therefore all progress depends on the unreasonable man.'

1.
Night and the railway

Left My first sight of the Great Western was in 1949. I had just arrived from Australia and on that first night I made my way to Paddington Station. What I saw then was very much like this 1960 scene - 'Castles' and 'Halls' and a 'King' or two were there. Here we see 'Castle' Class No 7021 *Haverfordwest Castle* waiting to run down to Old Oak Common Shed.

Below On New Year's Eve 1962 I made an attempt to emulate top American railroad photographer W. O. Winston Link by trying to get a lineside action shot at night using flash. Here 'Castle' Class No 5087 *Tintern Abbey* is caught in the glare of two big PF100 flashbulbs just outside Twyford as she is about to enter Sonning Cutting. Her leaky inside steam pipe joint helped produce a spectacular picture.

Left Motive Power Depots were the base for both engines and crew. Working conditions were never ideal but in spite of the dirty, dark and smoky conditions prevailing, many railwaymen remember them with great affection. Of course, to the enthusiastic they were the epitome of steam railway atmosphere. Here at Reading WR Shed on a frosty January night in 1961, two 'Hall' Class 4-6-0s simmer quietly on No 9 Through Road. The running sheds are clearly seen in the background.

Below left A 'Prairie' tank and a 'Hall' standing outside the main running shed at Reading evoke all the atmosphere of a Great Western steam shed. The 2-6-2Ts in one form or another were the mainstay of both London suburban and branch-line duties throughout the system.

This page Fireman Eddie Robinson of Reading Shed sweeps ash off the front footplate and fills the oil head-lamp of 'Modified Hall' No 6989 *Wightwick Hall* in preparation for a late-night shift. At that time *Wightwick Hall* was based at Worcester (85A). She was withdrawn in June 1964 and is preserved at Quainton Road.

Left Inside the running shed '4300' Class 2-6-0 No 6385 from Exeter rests near a brazier giving out welcome light and heat. The 'Mogul' was a Churchward design going back to 1911.

Centre left Nearby, fitters have found a fault which needs attention in 'Hall' Class 4-6-0 No 5906 *Lawton Hall*, a Reading-based loco. A conference is in progress.

Below left *Lawton Hall*'s problem was diagnosed as being a defective cylinder head stud. Reading Fitter Eric Hall (left) is drilling out the faulty stud, helped by Fitter George Stares. The replacement stud can be seen on the front footplate close to the left-hand end of the spanner.

Right Meanwhile 'Hall' Class 4-6-0 No 5999 *Wollaton Hall*, visiting from Westbury, slumbers peacefully nearby. She will not be lit up until tomorrow. No 5999 was withdrawn in September 1962 and scrapped at Swindon a couple of months later.

2.
Some stations

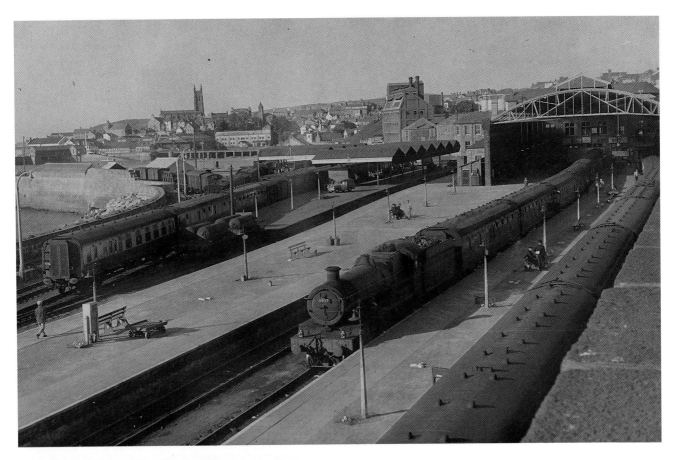

Above Stations, large and small, were favourite spots for enthusiasts in steam days. This is the end of the GWR line at Penzance in the summer of 1959. Penzance-based 'Grange' 4-6-0 No 6837 *Forthampton Grange* waits to leave with a down express. No 6837 survived to July 1965 but was scrapped in October of that year at Birds, Swansea.

Left King's Cross, also in 1959, and two locomotives having recently arrived with up expresses wait to follow their coaches out of the station platforms. On the right is 'A3' 'Pacific' No 60110 *Robert the Devil* while on the left is the unique 'W1' Class 4-6-4 (or more accurately 4-6-2-2) No 60700 which was a conventional three-cylinder rebuild of Gresley's 1929 experimental 'Hush-hush' four-cylinder compound high-pressure locomotive fitted with a water-tube boiler. The 'W1' as originally built carried the number 10000; it was not really successful but was useful publicity for the LNER. No 60700 was withdrawn in 1959, but the original water-tube boiler supplied test steam in the Stooperdale shop at Darlington Works right up to 1966.

Right At King's Cross in steam days, visiting locomotives did not need necessarily to visit Top Shed for servicing, as a small Depot was tucked in to the west side of the station. It was complete with a turntable, here seen turning Thompson 'A2/3' 'Pacific' No 60523 *Sun Castle*. *Courtesy British Railways*

Right There was also a small coaling machine, seen here refilling the tender of Haymarket-based 'A4' 'Pacific' No 60009 *Union of South Africa* which has just brought in the 'Elizabethan' non-stop from Edinburgh. No 60009 is now preserved at Markinch, Fife, Scotland. For political reasons she ran for a while as *Osprey*, but it is reported that she has been seen bearing her original name.

Right In 1961 'A3' 'Pacific' No 60039 *Sandwich*, fitted with double chimney and German-type smoke deflectors, arrives at King's Cross with an express from Newcastle. By this time the 'A3s' and 'A4s' were enjoying an Indian Summer; fitting double blastpipes and chimneys at very moderate cost had really transformed their performance and they were the mainstay of express services on the East Coast route right up to the end of steam. Today the old signal box on the right has of course vanished and electric wires are an established part of the scene.

Left Two Peppercorn 'A1' 'Pacifics' newly arrived at King's Cross in 1959 - on the left is No 60131 *Osprey* from Copley Hill (56C), while on the right is Doncaster-based No 60156 *Great Central*. The latter was one of the five 'A1s' fitted with Timken roller-bearings on all axleboxes; the greater cost was more than compensated for by trouble-free running and greater time between major overhauls. No Peppercorn 'Pacific' was preserved, but there is currently a scheme to build a new one from scratch, a plan that appears to be attracting much support.

Left Another King's Cross pairing. 'A3' 'Pacific' No 60061 *Pretty Polly* heads the 'Heart of Midlothian' a few minutes before departure in the summer of 1961. No 60061 has a double chimney which was fitted in 1958, and very small smoke deflectors on each side of the chimney; her German-type deflectors were not fitted until the end of 1961. The 'Heart of Midlothian' was the early afternoon express to Edinburgh, leaving King's Cross at 1.00 pm. The service dated back to the first decade of the century and was one of the last Great Northern expresses to use a slip coach, which was released at Doncaster. On the left is Thompson 2-6-4T 'L1' Class No 67776 on station pilot duties, which they shared with the ubiquitous 'N2' 0-6-2Ts one of which, No 69504, is seen here (*above*). These highly successful tank locos were a development by Gresley of an earlier Great Northern design. Many based in the London area were

fitted with condensing gear for working suburban services underground on the so-called 'Widened Lines'. No 69523 of this class is preserved; it operates as LNER No 4744 and is owned by the Gresley Society.

Right 'A1/1' Class No 60113 *Great Northern* was another unique 'Pacific'; it was a complete rebuild of the then Class 'A10' 'Pacific' *Great Northern*, Nigel Gresley's original Great Northern 'Pacific', and its rebuild caused much controversy.

Above 'A3' 'Pacific' No 60066 *Merry Hampton*, with double chimney but no smoke deflectors as yet, waits to take out an afternoon departure from King's Cross for Peterborough. She looks as if she may be leaking a little steam from an inside joint. How often in those days did one walk up to the head end 'to look at the engine' before taking a trip!

Left Indeed, King's Cross station was a veritable paradise for spotters!

Above Euston was almost as good as King's Cross but it was rather more enclosed. Here 'Princess Coronation' Class 'Pacific' No 46228 *Duchess of Rutland* waits to leave with an express for North Wales. No 46228 was one of the original streamlined 'Pacifics'; she was withdrawn in 1964 and scrapped at Cashmores, Great Bridge, in the same year. Departures from Euston were often spectacular. The grade up to the Regents Canal was 1 in 68 and 1 in 77, so locomotives on heavy expresses had to work hard, even with the usual push from the tank engine which had brought in the coaches. To lighten the load tenders would often be only half full of water - to be topped up at Bushey Troughs.

Right The 'Manxman' has arrived at Euston behind rebuilt 'Royal Scot' 4-6-0 No 46142 *The York and Lancaster Regiment*. The 'Manxman' carried this name in summer because the service connected at Liverpool with Isle of Man boat services. On the left is one of the Southern Region's first attempts at diesel-electric traction, No 10201 built at Ashford in 1950.

Ready to leave Euston at the head of the 8:50 am express to Birmingham on 28 June 1957 is rebuilt 'Patriot' Class 4-6-0 No 45532 *Illustrious*. When they first appeared, the 'Patriots' were known as 'Baby Scots' because they closely resembled their bigger sisters the 'Royal Scots', and many finished their days in original condition. None was preserved.

Above Another London station where Eastern Region 'A3' 'Pacifics' could be seen was Marylebone. Here Leicester-based 'A3' No 60107 *Royal Lancer* prepares to return home with a down express in 1957. The crew (on the left) appear to be discussing some aspect of No 60107's condition. On 1 May 1928 *Royal Lancer*, together with No 4472 *Flying Scotsman*, inaugurated the non-stop 'Flying Scotsman' service. She departed from Edinburgh with the up train at 10.00 am at the same moment as *Flying Scotsman* pulled out of King's Cross.

Right Out of town, York Station was always a delight to visit - the great through train shed was beautiful. In this 1963 picture one of the first production 'Deltics' hurries the 'Flying Scotsman' through the down middle road on a cold, wet day. Nowadays the station is a shadow of its former self and has lost the two middle roads. The 'Deltic' - and all her sisters - have also passed into history although, of course, several are preserved.

Above At the eastern end of Reading West Station there were - indeed still are - a couple of platforms used by Southern Region third-rail electrics, which ran to and from Waterloo. However, on occasion the Southern's steam services to Redhill and beyond via Guildford used the platforms. Here in 1961 a train to Tonbridge is about to leave headed by 'U' Class 2-6-0 No 31627. This Guildford-based loco was not one of the 'Us' to survive into preservation.

Left Diesels were also working expresses through Reading West on the Western Region, but they were diesel-hydraulics. Here a 'Warship' approaches with an up express while Castle Class 4-6-0 No 7027 *Thornbury Castle*, heading a Paddington-Bristol express, waits for the starting signal (on the left). *Thornbury Castle* is showing a slight drift of steam from the inside cylinder exhaust steam pipe. She was withdrawn in December 1963 and happily is preserved by the Standard Gauge Steam Trust. The diesel-hydraulics are also gone now, but again several have been preserved in full working order.

3.
Servicing a 'Royal Scot' at Camden

Left The entrance to the London Midland Region's Shed at Camden, just outside Euston, was near Chalk Farm Station in Dumpton Place off Gloucester Road. It was an extremely cramped place - as can be seen, a 'Princess Coronation' 'Pacific' is dropping down between the gate and the office entrance towards the ash plant.

Below These pictures were taken on Wednesday 12 August 1959. In this general view of the north end of the shed the approach road is seen on the extreme left. In front of the shed are, from the left, 'Jubilee' 4-6-0 No 45553 *Canada*, Class '5' 4-6-0 No 44948, 'Royal Scot' 4-6-0 No 46148 *The Manchester Regiment*, and 'Jubilee' 4-6-0 No 45703 *Thunderer*.

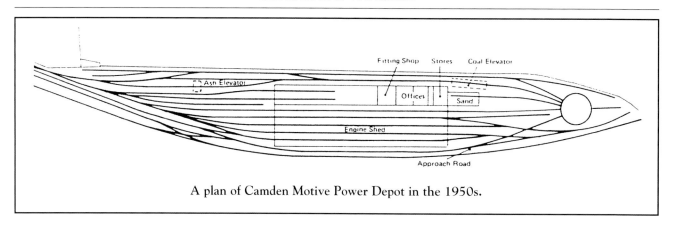

A plan of Camden Motive Power Depot in the 1950s.

Arriving on the approach road and backing towards the turntable is 'Royal Scot' Class 4-6-0 No 46126 *Royal Army Service Corps*. The Carlisle-based 'Scot' has just brought in the 'Northern Irishman' and is visiting Camden for servicing. Notice how close the local housing was to the shed - no wonder there were continual complaints about smoke. Loco tenders were always supplied with a modicum of coke at Camden in an attempt to reduce smoke emissions.

Above The turntable was not only used for turning engines but also 'switched' locomotives from the approach road to the appropriate shed road (see the plan opposite). It was vacuum operated and here No 46126 is turning herself. Interestingly, No 46126 was star of the 1949 movie *Train of Events*. The film deals with various human dramas leading up to a train crash. In the first sequences showing the locomotive arriving at Willesden Shed and being stabled there, the last digit of her number has been painted out - just why is not really known. The suggestion that it may have been a desire not to identify the locomotive as it is wrecked later on does not hold water because the full number is clearly seen when the locomotive backs down on to the coaches of her train at Euston just prior to departure. Jack Warner plays a very convincing top link driver and looks exactly right in the part. *Train of Events* is a film warmly recommended to railway enthusiasts.

Right To take the next locomotive the turntable had to be returned to the approach road by hand - here it is being cranked round.

Royal Army Service Corps now has to queue for her turn to take coal and water. The wait over, No 46126's tender is filled under the coaling plant. Note the coal wagon being lifted up on the left to have its contents automatically tipped into the plant's hopper. If you look carefully you can see pieces of coal dropping down into the tender.

Right Next No 46126 is watered; her tender has been somewhat overfilled before the water was turned off.

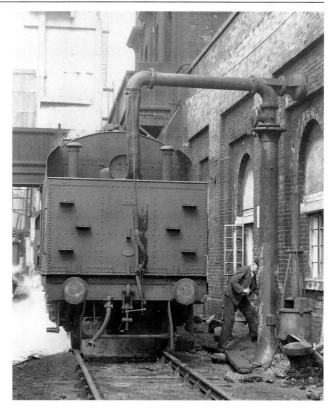

Below Now *Royal Army Service Corps* passes under Camden's ash plant. Normally hot ash was efficiently removed by narrow gauge trucks running in the pits between the rails. On this occasion, however, the ash plant was out of action and the trucks and pits were themselves badly choked with ash.

Things certainly were in a mess that day! Nearby another visitor, 'Britannia' Class 'Pacific' No 70033 *Charles Dickens* from Longsight, Manchester (9A), looks disdainfully on while shed staff attempt to clear some of the mountains of ash.

Next No 46126's hopper ash pan doors are opened, then the fire is racked over the ash pits. After that comes perhaps one of the dirtiest jobs of all - shovelling out accumulated ash from the smokebox.

Left Cleaning should follow, but as Camden's usual complement of 32 cleaners was then reduced to just two, No 46126 will have to wait until she returns to her home shed later in the day, and will have to be contented with a little oiling instead.

Right The Engine Working Arrangements board at Camden showed all planned engine movements at the MPD for that day. The second entry from the top in the second 'Passenger' column on the left shows that '6126' *Royal Army Service Corps* will return northwards on the 4.55 pm express to Blackpool. In August 1959 there were 45 steam locomotives allocated to Camden, but this had dwindled to four when the shed finally closed on 9 September 1963; the survivors were transferred to Willesden and all remaining traces of the shed were demolished in 1964. No 46126 was withdrawn in October 1963, and scrapped in November at Crewe Works.

4.
Top Shed, King's Cross

King's Cross Motive Power Depot - 'Top Shed' - was located in the heart of King's Cross Goods Yard. It could not be seen from the roads nearby, but there was an excellent panoramic view to be had from passing North London Line trains. This 1959 view was taken from the top of the coaling plant, and shows a line-up of locomotives in front of the running shed which dated back to Great Northern days. Just behind the running shed the arches of the original depot, built around 1850, can be seen, where repair work was carried out right up to the end. The trucks on the left are partially filled with ash removed from the adjacent pits. Over to the right the water gantry can be seen. *Courtesy British Railways*

Left The entrance to Top Shed's offices. The weather vane, made of sheet brass, was in the form of an Ivatt large-boilered 'Atlantic', and is reputed nowadays to grace a farm building 'somewhere in England'.

Right As at most sheds, turning was the first priority. Here 'B1' Class 4-6-0 No 61096 runs on to the turntable at Top Shed after having brought one of the 'Cambridge Buffet Expresses' into King's Cross; she will be serviced here before returning to Cambridge, her home base. The 'B1' two-cylinder 4-6-0s were designed by Edward Thompson and appeared in 1942. They replaced many aging GNR 'Atlantics' on the LNER; two have been preserved and are based at Loughborough.

Below right Turning the 'B1' is the Deputy Foreman at Top Shed, Driver J. McArthur. Note the connection from the locomotive's vacuum pipe to the turntable's vacuum motor apparatus. On the left, two 'N2' tanks are coming on shed, bypassing the turntable. No 69578 has been on suburban duties and carries a 'Broad Street' headboard.

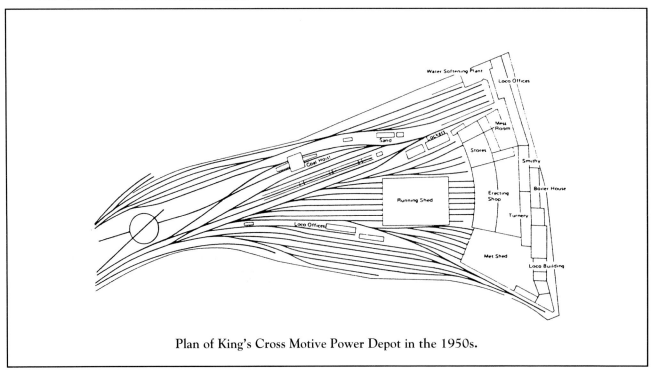

Plan of King's Cross Motive Power Depot in the 1950s.

Right In modern coaling plants like that at Top Shed, coal trucks were automatically lifted up the side of the tower and their contents dumped before the empty truck was returned to the track below. In this sequence we first of all see the full truck on its way up. Next the truck starts to tip at the top of the tower, then over she goes and the coal is tipped into the plant.

New England '9F' 2-10-0 No 92041 takes on coal beneath the coaling plant. The 2-10-0 bears the letters 'SC' on her smokebox door, indicating that she has a self-cleaning smokebox, a device that was beginning to make engine maintenance work less unpleasant.

By contrast, 'V2' 2-6-2 No 60871, over the ash pits, is having a great deal of accumulated ash raked and shovelled out of her smokebox. Eleven 'V2s' were allocated to Top Shed at that time, and this was one of them.

Left After the ash has been dealt with, No 60871 has her fire raked out.

Below left This little steam shovel was used at Top Shed to remove ash and clinker from the ash pits and transfer it to waiting wagons.

Above right A large water gantry spanning several tracks was a feature of Top Shed, and meant that at busy times a number of locomotives could be watered simultaneously.

Right Early afternoon outside the running shed at Top Shed could offer an exciting view. There, waiting to run down to King's Cross Station, could often be seen several immaculately groomed locomotives ready to haul the important afternoon departures on the East Coast Main Line. Here Chargehand Cleaner Dick Ball stands proudly by 'A4' No 60017 *Silver Fox*, next to which simmers quietly No 60008 *Dwight D. Eisenhower* and No 60013 *Dominion of New Zealand*. *Silver Fox* and *Dominion of New Zealand* are sadly no more, but *Dwight D. Eisenhower* is preserved at the American National Railroad Museum, Wisconsin, USA.

A little behind the trio of 'A4s' seen on the previous page, a variety of engines were to be seen at the front of the running shed, including 'A2' 'Pacific' No 60513 *Dante*, 'A1' 'Pacific' No 60157 *Great Eastern*, and a glimpse of 'A4' 'Pacific' No 60006 *Sir Ralph Wedgwood*.

Right Headboards for the expresses on the East Coast route were kept in the entrance to the Running Shed Foreman's office. Except in a very few notable cases, the practice of naming trains has fallen out of favour - yet another attractive feature of the old railway which has vanished.

Below At Top Shed great store was set in turning out their locomotives in as smart a condition as possible. Here a gang of cleaners under the watchful eye of Chargehand Cleaner Dick Ball (right) spare no effort to make 'A1' Pacific No 60149 *Amadis* ready for the 'Tees-Tyne Pullman'. *Amadis* was a King's Cross loco but she moved to Doncaster (36A) in October 1958, where she stayed until withdrawn in June 1964. She was scrapped at Wards, Killamarsh, seven months later. The 'Tees-Tyne Pullman' with its 4.50 pm departure from King's Cross and bound for Newcastle, had started life as a successor in a way to the pre-war 'Silver Jubilee', but the only real similarities were the initial departure time of 5.30 pm from King's Cross and running non-stop to Darlington; the schedule was much slower than the old 'Silver Jubilee'.

Above Outside the running shed a little later on, Peter Townend, Shed Master of King's Cross at the time (left), is chatting to Chargehand Cleaner Dick Ball (right). In the middle was the then youngest member of the Shed staff, 15-year-old Brian Watts. Brian had just started work as a cleaner but would go on to learn to be a fireman, later a driver. To drive a passenger train meant a considerable number of years training and working through the grades. A learner driver in charge of a passenger train - even with an instructor present - is a practice on British Rail now rightly causing ASLEF some concern, and which was totally unheard of on our vanished railway.

Left An 'A1' has a fault in her sanding mechanism. As fitters work to rectify the fault, sand cascades down on to the track.

Right This 'V2' was in steam and due out of the shed in a couple of hours, but fitters were attending to an urgent problem in the motion. One of the difficulties experienced by BR towards the end of steam operations was that shed staff became more and more reluctant to work on locomotives while they were still hot.

However, BR Standard Class '5' No 73157 was cold and waits for the return of two pairs of her driving wheels.

Above Outside the 'Met Shed' at King's Cross MPD are two of the condenser-fitted 'N2' 0-6-2T engines. Top Shed had 52 'N2s' at the time; they handled most GN suburban services and did sterling work as station pilots, moving empty stock in and out of King's Cross Station. They could also be seen on many coal and goods trains in the area.

Left Inside the Met Shed a fitter takes a hammer to a recalcitrant brake rod under an 'N2'.

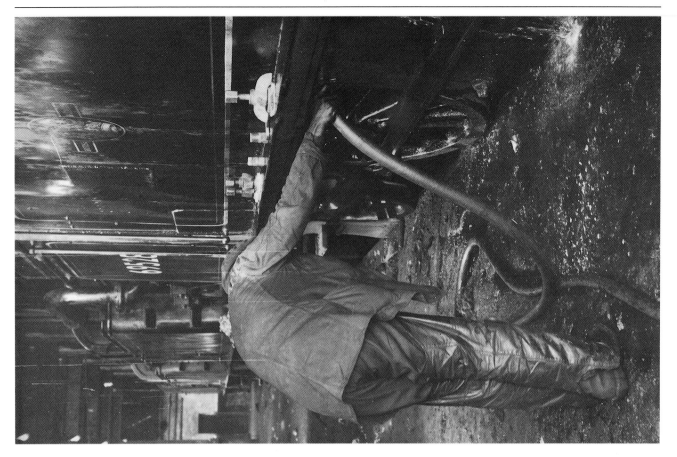

Nearby, another 'N2' has had one of her inside Stephenson's valve motion eccentrics removed for attention, while No 69528 has a boiler washout.

Left In the Erecting Shop behind the running shed at King's Cross, various locomotives were undergoing repair. Here an unidentified 'A4' has her smokebox door opened - the relationship between the streamlined front-end doors and the smokebox door is clearly shown. The detachable hand cranks which opened the streamlined doors were a constant worry to shed staff because they were very easily lost, especially in the vicinity of piles of ash.

Right Elsewhere in the Erecting Shop 'A4' 'Pacific' No 60034 *Lord Faringdon* is the subject for discussion between two fitters. Note the string of nuts and washers on a piece of wire hanging from the front running board and the piston rings on the buffers.

Below Also in the Erecting Shop was 'A3' 'Pacific' No 60062 *Minoru*; a fitter is working on her 'banjo' dome. The archway under which *Minoru* is standing was the front of the original running shed of the 1850s.

Right Behind the Erecting Shop were extensive workshop facilities. Prior to the construction of the new Crimpsall Erecting Shop at Doncaster in 1902, heavy repair of locomotives had been carried out at King's Cross MPD. Even at the time that these pictures were taken, quite extensive repair jobs were undertaken. Double blastpipes and chimneys were frequently fitted, and a big wheel lathe was part of the equipment. Here a pair of driving wheels from a three-cylinder 'Pacific' are installed ready for turning of a journal. Note the balanced crank which takes the connecting rod of the middle cylinder.

Left In another corner of the turnery, Gresley derived motion linkages are receiving attention, and connecting rods lie on a bench.

Right A small hydraulic press in the turnery is being used to punch out a bush from a coupling rod.

Below In the Smithy, Top Shed's blacksmith is shaping a brake rod. The fire is over to the right and all a blacksmith's tools of the trade can be seen hanging behind. We may well sigh nostalgically over the loss of the beloved steam engine but the real tragedy of the passing of steam was the irretrievable loss of so many arts, crafts and skills which vanished with the steam railway.

'A3' 'Pacific' No 60103 *Flying Scotsman* was certainly Top Shed's most famous inhabitant. *Flying Scotsman* was withdrawn from BR service in January 1963, and a few months later, on 7 June, Top Shed itself closed. The area was levelled and today absolutely no sign of that great establishment remains. *Flying Scotsman*, however, went on to many quite extraordinary adventures, none of which could have been dreamed of when this cleaner polished her buffer beam in King's Cross MPD's old running shed over 30 years ago.

5.
The Eastern Region
Steam Instruction Train

Left The former LNER Steam Instruction Train was a travelling school which regularly toured motive power depots throughout the Eastern and North Eastern Regions, and ex-LNER part of the Scottish Region. Here it is with Inspector and tutor in charge Mr McCluskey, at King's Cross MPD. Mr McCluskey is walking past the coach fitted up as a classroom complete with blackboard and other teaching aids.

Below The Instruction Train was a great help to railwaymen studying for the various exams which had to be passed in the climb up the promotion ladder. Inspector McCluskey is seen here teaching a group in the train's classroom.

Left The Instruction Train was fitted out with many superb working models and cut-away examples of steam railway equipment. Here are seen models of Stephenson's link motion valve gear.

Below left Inspector McCluskey, using a fully detailed working model, explains how the Gresley two-to-one valve gear operates. His students are two King's Cross fireman coming up for examination. On the left is Junior Driver Tony Blaxill, a life-long railway enthusiast, and now himself a Southern Region Instructor.

Below right During a visit to an MPD, the exhibits on the train were always available for private study. Here a group examine the features of a vacuum brake ejector.

Above In this part of the Instruction Train large cut-away parts of brake systems were exhibited. Illuminated, fully detailed diagrams set in the roof gave further information.

Right Here we see the section of the train dealing with how the boiler is supplied with water. On the wall is a diagram of an exhaust steam injector and, immediately below, the real thing is shown in cut-away form.

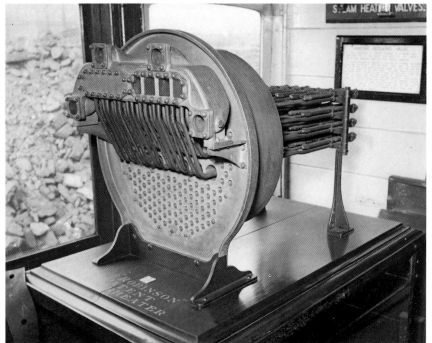

Above Amongst the many beautiful models was this striking exhibit showing a complete boiler and firebox.

Left The LNER Steam Instruction Train largely dated back to the heyday of the Great Northern Railway but it was, of course, added to and expanded in LNER days. This model of the Robinson Patent Superheater was inherited from the Great Northern. When steam died, the Instruction Train was broken up. Many of its best exhibits can be seen at the National Railway Museum, but, like so much else of the railway scene, the Steam Instruction Train has vanished.

6.
Old Oak Common Shed

Old Oak Common was the GWR's biggest steam shed. It had been designed by Churchward and measured 444 feet by 360 feet. Inside the Great Shed were four 65-foot turntables, each with 28 radiating roads making up a total of 112 engine pits. It was the first of the GWR's internal turntable depots and was the prototype for many others, but none was as big. In this 1961 picture the running sheds are over to the right and the brick arches of the 1 in 50 ramp approach to the coal stage are visible on the extreme right. The water columns are still fitted with old-style leather bags and the '4300' Class 'Mogul' adjacent to the second water column has a 3,000-gallon tender - probably borrowed temporarily.

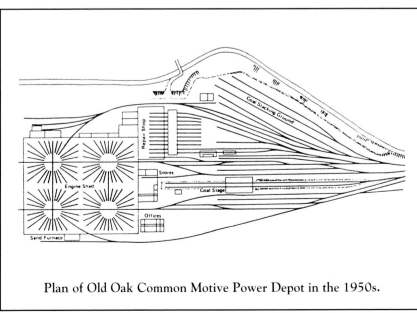

Plan of Old Oak Common Motive Power Depot in the 1950s.

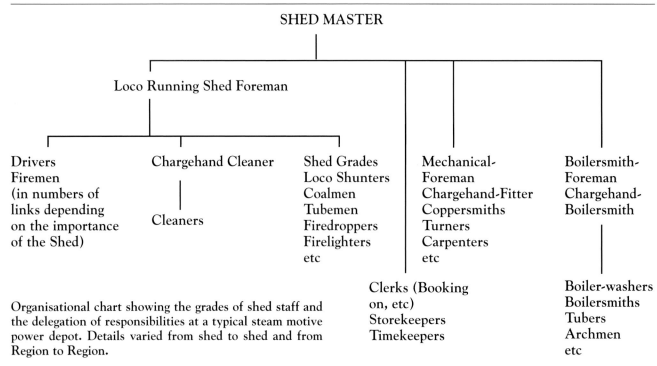

SHED MASTER

Loco Running Shed Foreman

Drivers Firemen (in numbers of links depending on the importance of the Shed)	Chargehand Cleaner	Shed Grades Loco Shunters Coalmen Tubemen Firedroppers Firelighters etc	Mechanical-Foreman Chargehand-Fitter Coppersmiths Turners Carpenters etc	Boilersmith-Foreman Chargehand-Boilersmith
	Cleaners			

Clerks (Booking on, etc)
Storekeepers
Timekeepers

Boiler-washers
Boilersmiths
Tubers
Archmen
etc

Organisational chart showing the grades of shed staff and the delegation of responsibilities at a typical steam motive power depot. Details varied from shed to shed and from Region to Region.

The coaling stage at Old Oak Common had elevated supply lines (on the brick arches in the previous picture) and was the largest on the GWR. On top of it was a vast 290,000-gallon water tank. The GWR did not favour mechanical coaling plants, preferring instead to use tip wagons which had been hand-filled like the one emptying coal into the tender of 'Castle' Class No 5045 *Earl of Dudley*. In this way exactly the right kind of supply could be ensured for each locomotive class. A 'Castle' like this would get good-sized pieces of first-quality Welsh coal.

Above While coaling is going on, No 5045's smokebox is being cleaned. If you have ever wondered what was the purpose of the small cock on the front of the smokeboxes of GWR locomotives, you can see it here in use - a hose was connected to it so that a jet of steam and water could be used to aid the cleaning process and make it less unpleasant. Just behind is 'Castle' Class No 5049 *Earl of Plymouth* from St Philip's Marsh, Bristol (82A). She is in a hurry and will leave the shed today very shortly after servicing. The service point at Ranelagh Yard at Paddington was very busy that Saturday, otherwise she would have been dealt with there.

Left Earl of Plymouth is now dropping down quickly for the short run to Paddington Station to take out an express for Bristol.

Left Before hurrying off, No 5049 *Earl of Plymouth* had been turned inside the Great Shed like No 5045 *Earl of Dudley*, now having her turn while a fitter and the shed driver have a chat.

Below A line-up of resting steam in the Great Shed. Included in this shot are, from the left, 'Castle' Class No 4076 *Carmarthen Castle*, one of the original 'Castles' built in 1924, 'King' Class No 6029 *King Edward VIII*, 'Grange' Class No 6856 *Stowe Grange*, and 'Castle' Class No 5046 *Earl Cawdor*.

Above Boiler blow-down for 'Castle' Class No 5014 *Goodrich Castle*. On the far left is a shed fitter's portable work-bench with, alongside, a fitter's barrow with a hollow for carrying valves.

Below Another fitter's portable workbench stands in front of 'King' Class No 6012 *King Edward VI*, a long-time Old Oak Common-based engine.

An Old Oak Common fire-lighter (*above left*), his shovel filled with special bundles of wood and oily cotton waste, makes ready to light up the fire of a 'Castle'. In GWR days he was called a 'lighter-up'. (*Above right*) Into the firebox goes the bundle of wood. The lighter-up knows that it will take about 5 hours to raise steam in a 'Castle', and 3 hours for smaller locos. In addition to lighting fires, the lighter-up will keep an eye on other engines in steam, regularly checking their water levels, steam pressures and the state of their fires.

Left There was, and indeed still is, a very well-equipped repair shop at Old Oak Common, but it is now, of course, fitted out for work on diesel-electric locomotives and HSTs. The Great Shed has vanished but one of the turntables still remains. However, when this picture was taken steam still reigned supreme and 'Castle' Class No 5071 *Spitfire*, a visitor from Gloucester (85B), has had her front pair of driving wheels and pony truck removed. The built-up crank axle driven by the two inside cylinders can be clearly seen. These axles were made at Swindon of nine separate components which were hydraulically pressed together and then keyed.

Right Outside the repair shop is a line-up of 'Castles' and 'Halls'; nearest the camera is No 5053 *Earl Cairns*.

Above Meanwhile, on a nearby road stands 'King' Class No 6010 *King Charles I* waiting to be lit up early on Monday morning.

Left The ubiquitous pannier tank 0-6-0PTs were everywhere on the GWR, particularly so at Paddington where they could be seen moving stock in and out of the station. No 8757 was a slightly modified version of the original Collett 1929 '5700' design, dating back to 1933. Several of these pannier tanks have been preserved, but No 8757 was not one of them. A few, Nos 9700-10, were fitted with condensing apparatus for working over the Metropolitan Line.

Right Fuelled, watered, turned and cleaned, now 'Castle' Class No 5045 *Earl of Dudley* simmers gently outside the Great Shed waiting her next turn of duty and return to her home shed at Wolverhampton. She had only a few more years left in service, being withdrawn in September 1962 and scrapped at Cox & Danks, Langley Green, Oldbury, that very same month.

Below Soon No 5045 will follow 'Castle' Class No 5065 *Newport Castle* off shed. *Newport Castle* is due to haul the 'Red Dragon', leaving Paddington for Swansea at 5.55 pm. The ringed signals were used on the Western Region as yard exit signals. As we can see here, their movement was somewhat limited and drivers would complain that it was often hard to see when they were off.

As No 5065 pulls away past Old Oak Common Engine Shed Signal Box into the sunset, we reluctantly say farewell (almost) to Old Oak Common Shed, parts of which still remain - but certainly goodbye to *Newport Castle*, which vanished under the scrapper's torch at Kings, Norwich, in December 1963.

7.
Willesden Shed

Above Big steam locomotive depots were busy places - they not only looked after their own locomotives, but they also had to service visiting engines. Willesden MPD (1A), dating back to London & North Western days, was home to 130 locos in 1959 - even in 1965 there were 67 engines there. In this 1962 photograph the crew are preparing 'Jubilee' Class 4-6-0 No 45600 *Bermuda* - note the oilcans in the left foreground and on the running board of the 'Jubilee'. On the left is 'Britannia' Class 'Pacific' No 70021 *Morning Star*, on the right is 'Britannia' No 70054 *Dornoch Firth*, and on the far right little BR Standard Class '2' 2-6-0 No 78033. Several of these Class '2s' are preserved, but No 78033 was not among them.

Right Stanier 'Black Five' 4-6-0 No 45187 stands in front of two engine-men sitting on a rail for a chat at Willesden Shed on a summer Saturday afternoon in 1962. The 'Black Fives' were amongst the most successful and popular steam locomotives ever built. Over ten have been preserved and they were the last class to survive in any significant numbers by 1967.

Above 'Princess Coronation', or 'Duchess', Class 'Pacific' No 46254 *City of Stoke on Trent* (one of the class not originally streamlined) takes on coal under the coaling plant at Willesden Shed. She had a couple of years left before withdrawal in October 1964; she was cut up at Cashmores, Great Bridge, two months later.

Left Another view of *City of Stoke on Trent* over the ash pits. Willesden MPD had a covered turntable in the roundhouse, and in the film *Train of Events* there are some most evocative scenes taken in the roundhouse showing the stabling of 'Royal Scot' 4-6-0 No 46126 *Royal Army Service Corps* (see also page 28).

An interesting line-up of locomotives at Willesden; on the left is resident 'Patriot' Class 4-6-0 No 45538 *Giggleswick* in original unrebuilt form. Many were rebuilt with larger taper boilers like the 'Royal Scots', but the original 'Patriots' were good-looking engines and - dare I say it - I also preferred the original 'Royal Scots' to the rebuilds; they really did give the impression of power. No 'Patriots' were preserved and No 45538 vanished at Crewe a few months after this picture was taken. 'Black Five' No 45256 next to it fared no better. '4F' 0-6-0 No 44497, last in line, was a member of a very large class of goods engines dating back to the early 1920s. As can be seen in this and other pictures, Willesden was a well-lit shed, but it closed is doors to steam in 1965 and like so much else of the old railway has now vanished.

8.
Nine Elms Shed

Left Nine Elms Shed (70A) was the very last main-line shed in the London area to close. It was situated just off the main line between Vauxhall and Queens Road Station, and one could get a good view of it from suburban services in and out of Waterloo. Today the whole site is occupied by the relocated Covent Garden Market. In this 1964 picture 'Q' Class 0-6-0 No 30545 has just come on shed and is running gently into the MPD after turning.

Below Another arrival at the shed is rebuilt 'Merchant Navy' Class 'Pacific' No 35019 *French Line CGT*, which has just come up from Southampton. The rebuilt 'West Country' and 'Merchant Navy' locomotives were much preferred by enginemen to the original Bulleid designs with their troublesome chain-driven valve gear and their generally difficult accessibility for servicing.

Above Another 'Merchant Navy', No 35020 *Bibby Line*, is over the ash pits having her fire raked out.

Right The valve gear of 'Merchant Navy' 'Pacific' No 35001 *Channel Packet* in rebuilt form gives a little concern to a shed driver and fitter at Nine Elms. *Channel Packet* was the first of Bulleid's 'Merchant Navy' Class. Appearing in 1941 in 'air-smoothed' sheathing and with the special Bulleid valve gear, she was numbered 21C-1 and was an advance in steam locomotive design. All the class were subsequently rebuilt with Walschaerts valve gear and with the air-smoothed casing removed.

A trio of rebuilt Bulleid 'Pacifics' stand on the ash pits outside the Old Running Shed at Nine Elms. This building dated back to 1885 and the New Shed, the roof of which is just seen on the right, was built in 1910. 'Battle of Britain' Class 'Pacific' No 34058 *Sir Frederick Pile* is just about to move off, while shed staff are shovelling up and removing ash.

Right Inside the Old Running Shed 'Pacifics' are receiving attention. In the foreground is 'West Country' Class No 34007 *Wadebridge* while in the background just coming in is No 34038 *Lynton*.

Below At Nine Elms the exit road from the coaling plant had a slight upward gradient and the rails were often wet and greasy. The Bulleid 'Pacifics', never too sure-footed at the best of times, would often slip and fuss when moving out, a sight which always gave much delight to shed visitors. Here 'West Country' 'Pacific' No 34103 *Calstock* is being coaled and will shortly attempt to move off.

9.
Reading Southern Shed

Reading Southern Shed was a delightful place. In 1962 it had just been made a sub-shed of Guildford and although it had no loco allocation of its own, but many types visited it. It was typical of many small sheds throughout the Southern Region. The small brick three-road shed on the right in this picture was built by the South Eastern Railway in the 1850s. Over the ash pit on the left is 'S15' Class 4-6-0 No 30500, an LSWR Urie design dating back to 1920. The Urie S15 Preservation Society has No 30506, but No 30500 is among those which vanished.

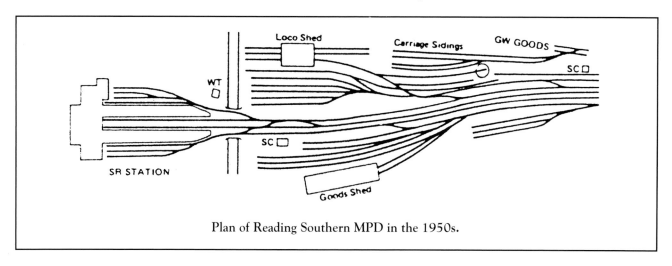

Plan of Reading Southern MPD in the 1950s.

Above Guildford-based 'U' Class 2-6-0 No 31631 is being turned manually by her driver and fireman on arrival at Reading Southern MPD. This locomotive was one of the 'U' Class engines built as such in 1928, but the class had originated as rebuilds of the ill-fated Maunsell SE&CR 'River' Class 2-6-4Ts. There is today some doubt about whether the causes of the Sevenoaks accident of 1927 really did justify the complete rebuilding of what had been a handsome and effective tank locomotive.

Right Inside the shed Maunsell-designed 'N' Class 'Mogul' No 31861 stands next to the shed offices while rather dimly in the background stands 'U' Class No 31808, one of the rebuilds of the original 'River' Class tanks.

The smaller, indeed older, Southern locomotives were good-looking engines and could appear very impressive, as 'N' Class 2-6-0 No 31820 demonstrates, seen resting at Reading Southern Shed. This was a Redhill locomotive and had brought in a train on the Tonbridge, Redhill, Guildford and Reading line. The line between Reading and Redhill had been built by the Reading, Guildford & Reigate Railway Company and was bought by the South Eastern Railway in 1852.

Above There were few mechanical aids at Reading Southern Shed. Coaling was done by hand and here 'N' Class 'Mogul' No 31864 is seen standing at the coaling platform - a shovel full of coal is clearly seen flying through the air on its way to the tender.

Below No 30690, in the centre of the trio of locomotives seen here outside the shed, was one of the Class '700' Drummond-designed 0-6-0s known as 'Black Motors' by railwaymen; 28 were still around as late as 1960. No 30690 was based at Guildford. On the left is 'U' Class 31625, now privately owned and living on the Mid-Hants Railway. On the right, No 31633, another 'U', did not survive, nor did Reading Shed, which closed in January 1965. On 5 April of that year Reading South Station itself closed when Southern Region operations in and out of Reading were all transferred to Reading General (WR) Station. The station and shed sites are now occupied by car parks and office buildings.

10.
Preparing a 'Castle' for duty

Above left It is a fine morning in 1961 and Driver Jack Gardner, based at Reading WR Motive Power Depot (81D), arrives for duty. His locomotive, 'Castle' Class No 5076 *Gladiator*, is already in steam and awaiting her driver and fireman.

Above right After first booking on duty, Jack collects some kit and oil cans from his locker.

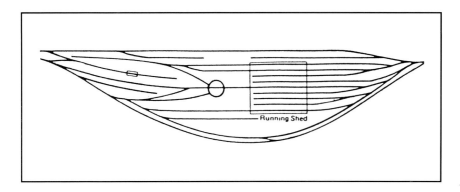

Plan of Reading (WR) Motive Power Depot in the 1950s. The shed was opened around 1880. Situated in the fork of the main lines to Bristol and Plymouth, it replaced the original broad gauge shed which had been sited directly opposite the station. Originally there was a turntable inside the running shed but this was moved outside in 1930 and the shed became a straight through one. It closed in January 1965.

At the stores (*right*) Jack collects cylinder lubricating oil; the small can contains paraffin and, a larger can, still to be passed through, will contain general lubricating oil. He then takes his supplies and kit to the waiting locomotive (*below*).

First there is a thorough round of oiling. There were over 60 oiling points on a big steam locomotive like a 'Castle' and enginemen needed to know the location of every single one of them. In accordance with GWR practice Jack oils the tender points first before the engine; here (*left*) he attends to the axleboxes, then (*below*) he makes sure that the water scoop operating mechanism is lubricated. In the next section we will be looking at troughs and how they operated.

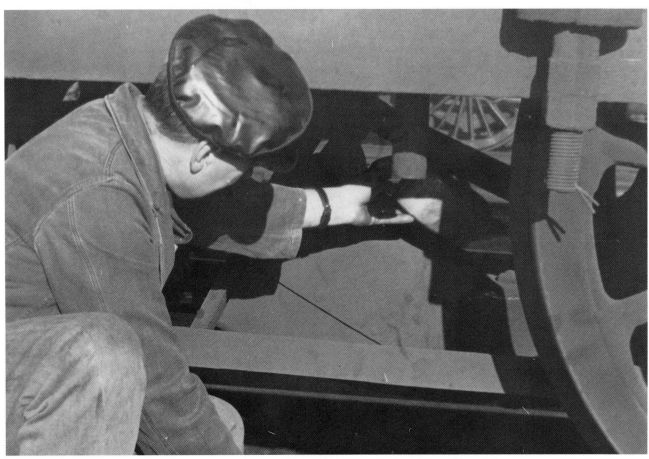

Right Here Jack is oiling the knuckle joint of the rocking arm to the inside valve spindle. In a 'Castle' the inside spindle drives the outside spindle through the rocking lever.

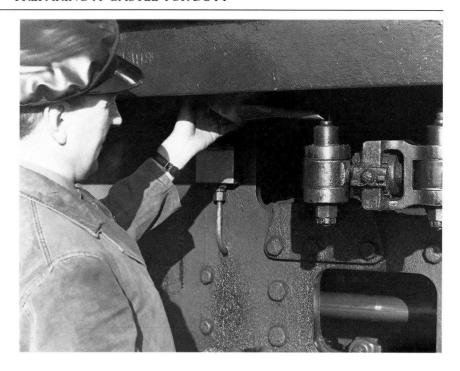

Below Here he is oiling the left-hand outside front-end valve spindle.

While Jack's fireman is getting up on the opposite side, Jack pulls the water column around to top up the tender. This column at Reading is fitted with the newer rubber flexible bag which replaced the old leather type we saw in use at Old Oak Common.

Finally Jack is ready to back *Gladiator* off shed and on to her train. That day No 5076 was diagrammed to work from Reading with the cross-country South of England to Birkenhead train, which shed staff called the 'Continental'. It had through coaches from Eastbourne, Hastings, Ramsgate, Margate, Folkestone, Deal, Dover, Sandwich and Brighton, had been assembled at Redhill, and was scheduled to depart from Reading at 1.07 pm. The service, the loco-motive and the shed have all now, sadly, vanished.

11.
Water troughs

Water troughs were invented in 1860 by John Ramsbottom so that steam locomotives could replenish their tenders without stopping. Troughs, 550 to 600 yards long, about 18 inches wide and 6 inches deep, were placed between the rails in a level section of track. In the heyday of steam there were 141 troughs in Britain - only the Southern Railway did not use them. The first troughs were installed at Mochdre on the Chester-Holyhead section of the London & North Western and were moved to Aber in 1871. The highest troughs in the world, at 1,169 feet above sea level, were at Garsdale on the Settle & Carlisle line. Water troughs near Diggle on the LNWR line between Manchester and Huddersfield were inside Standedge Tunnel - the only level section on the line - and overflow water was directed into the canal tunnel running alongside.

Left This set is at Bushey, near Watford on the London Midland Region, and is replenishing the tender of a down express. Although Bushey troughs were only 12 miles out of Euston, their presence meant that the load of heavy trains could be lightened to some extent for the climb up Camden Bank by starting them with half empty tenders, then filling them up at Bushey.

Above A closer view of the ramp into one end of a set of troughs at Bushey.

Right To be ready for the next train, which could be following within a few minutes, troughs had to be refilled very rapidly after the passage of a train. The water level was controlled by sensitive ball-and-valve arrangements and water was fed to the troughs at a number of points like the one shown here.

Above Adequate water supply tanks and water softening equipment were placed near troughs, as here at Bushey. Britain and America were the only countries to make extensive use of water troughs; in the States they were known as 'track pans'. The New York Central Railroad in particular made extensive use of them between Chicago and New York, the route of such famous expresses as the 'Twentieth Century Limited'.

Left Chemical treatment of water in softening plants meant that precipitated impurities in the water had to be removed as sludge. At Langley, north of King's Cross on the East Coast Main Line, old tenders, still in faded LNER livery, were used for this purpose. That nearest the camera bears the terse chalked instruction 'Empty you clots'!

Above The board on the right was the trackside warning to crews that they should lower the pick-up scoop. Here at Langley troughs the sign is about to be passed by a down express headed by 'A2/3' Class 'Pacific' No 60522 *Straight Deal* on her way home to York (50A).

Right Pick-up apparatus on the tender consisted of a curved pipe facing the front of the engine, to the lower end of which was fitted a scoop with a hinged joint. The scoop was 10 inches or so wide and dipped between $1\frac{1}{2}$ to $2\frac{1}{2}$ inches into the water when in its lowest position. Pictured here at Doncaster Works, such a scoop can be clearly seen.

Above At Langley troughs a passing train is replenishing its tender. The scoop can be plainly seen between the wheels with a small plume of spray just in front of it and with a wake behind. In order to lift water into the tender it was necessary to be travelling at 20 mph or more in order for the water to reach the necessary height. At a speed of 25 mph and with a dip of 2 inches, it was possible to take on 2,000 gallons when passing over a trough.

Left The resistance of the water against the scoop as it moved along was very great and lifting the scoop against this pressure was a hard job, as can be seen here on the footplate of 'A4' 'Pacific' No 60014 *Silver Link*. Some tenders were fitted with vacuum or steam assistance for lifting the scoop; in fact, experiments had shown that the entire drawbar pull of the locomotive could be absorbed by the scoop as it passed through a trough.

Above If tenders were reasonably full, picking up further water could result in a spectacular overflow like this one as 'A3' 'Pacific' No 60109 *Hermit* passes over Langley troughs with a down express. Unwary passengers in the first coach with open windows often got quite wet when this happened. As just mentioned, 2,000 gallons could be lifted at 25 mph, but the physics of the operation meant that at higher speeds the amount of water taken on did not increase significantly - but there was more spray and splash!

Right A footplate view approaching Werrington troughs on the East Coast Main Line from a rather leaky New England 'V2' 2-6-2, No 60867. Water troughs made possible long-distance non-stop running of steam locomotives; the non-stop 'Flying Scotsman' and its successor the 'Elizabethan' would have been impossible without them.

12.
Signals and signalmen

In the days of steam there were very many signal boxes. Each was manned by one or more signalmen and every signal box was in touch with other boxes on either side of it by an elaborate telegraph and telephone system.

Left For enginemen, a group of signals ahead meant that a signal box would soon be passed and you would shortly be waving to a friendly face at the signal box window. This is Willesden No 1 box just out of Euston on the LMR main line, with a down express about to rush by.

Left Another part of the duties of a signalman was to check every train as it went by, and he was the first person crews would contact if anything went wrong and a stop was necessary. When trains passed, signalmen often noticed things like 'hot boxes' (overheated axleboxes) and always checked that the tail lamp was in place and thus that the train was complete and through the section safely. At Willesden No 1 the signalman watches 'Jubilee' Class 4-6-0 No 45721 *Impregnable* running by light engine. Note the lamp placed in the light engine headcode position on the front footplate.

Part of a signalman's duties was to log every train which passed his box and to record fully details of any incidents. Here the signalman at Willesden makes an entry in his train register book.

Above There were numerous instruments in a signal box, mainly concerned with exchanging information regarding train movements within each signalman's 'block section'. Three-position block instruments were very common. Here the signalman at Willesden No 1 is changing the indication on a block instrument for the up main line. Indications would read 'Train on Line', 'Line Clear' or 'Line Blocked' (the latter being the normal state of the line, hence the term 'block section'), and the needle indication would be reproduced in the next signal box. In connection with the block instruments, signal boxes also communicated by a system of bell codes, Morse code-type telegraph keys being used. One 'ding' would call attention, then, for example, four 'dings' rung together would ask if the line was clear for an express. If so, the receiving signalman would repeat the code on his instrument. Details of the codes used have been published elsewhere, notably *British Railway Signalling* by G. M. Kichenside and A. Williams (Ian Allan).

On the right of the picture is a Train Describer. In order to avoid complicated bell codes, these had been developed from the early days. Setting the describer in one box produced a corresponding needle deflection in the next box. Here (*left*) is a close-up view of a describer at Willesden No 1 signal box. Indications include 'Goods for Broad St', 'Express for Euston', 'Special Passenger', 'Mails or Bullion', 'Light Engine for Camden Yard' and, punched in here, 'Fast Local to Euston'.

Above Reading West Main Signal Box was a very large and beautiful signal box in the old Great Western style. Here Signalman Blackall is operating the levers. In mechanical signal boxes, particularly where signals and points were some distance away, it required a good deal of strength to pull the levers. Of course, for some time powered movements of some signals and points had been introduced and colour-light signalling was, even in 1960, nothing new, but still mechanical signalling methods were by far the most common.

Right A system of 'track circuits' powered by accumulators and controlled by relays in the signal box provided information regarding train movements. Track diagrams with illuminated indicators such as this showing part of the layout at Reading West showed signalmen at a glance the position of trains on the line or in station platforms.

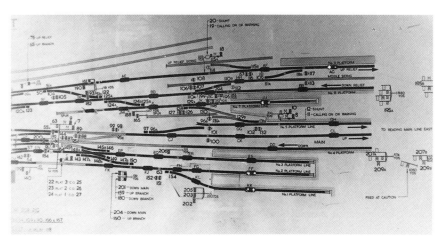

Opposite above Below the signal box operating floor was a veritable maze of wires, rods and other equipment. A complex and most reliable system of mechanical and electrical inter-locking prevented contra-indications and routing, and was installed under the signal box. Here Signalman Blackall inspects the mechanical interlocking.

Left Outside the signal box were numerous rods and wires leading off to the points and signals they controlled; the rods on the left operate points whereas the wires on the right go to semaphore signals.

Above left Just a part of the pulley system and linkages beneath the operating floor needed to operate signals by wire.

Above right Some of Reading West Main's signals took the form of shunting signals like this pair of disc ground signals, the faces of which rotated to give the clear indication.

Above Another means of signalmen communicating with one another was by telephone. Here one of Reading West Main's telephone sets is seen next to a three-position block instrument flanked by the tappers and bells communicating with the boxes on either side.

Left The Great Western Railway was the pioneer of Automatic Train Control in Britain. Information about the indications of a 'distant' (caution) signal at the approach to a section ahead is passed to the locomotive by means of a ramp set between the rails which engages with a shoe under the cab of the loco.

Below When the distant signal is at clear, a bell rings in the cab - the bell can be seen in front of the driver on the footplate of this 'Hall'. If the signal is at caution, a siren sounds and, if not acknowledged by the driver lifting a small handle on the apparatus, the brakes are automatically applied. The application of the brakes and the siren will continue until the driver acknowledges the signal.

Right The British Railways variant of this system uses magnetic inductors between the tracks like this one photographed on the Eastern Region main line out of King's Cross.

Below Under this system, when a distant signal is at caution a horn is sounded, the indicator in the cab changes to all black and the brakes are applied after a short delay. Acknowledging the indication with the handle on the apparatus releases the brakes and turns the indicator back to black and yellow as shown in this picture taken on the footplate of an ex-LNER 'A4' 'Pacific'. If the distant signal is clear, a bell rings in the cab for a short period.

Above The beautiful signal gantry at the west end of Reading General Station was controlled by Reading West Signal Box. In this picture 'Castle' Class 4-6-0 No 5090 *Neath Abbey* pulls away with a down express. The signals were, reading from left to right: up main line to up platform 5 home signal and, below it, up main line to up platform 5 inner distant signal worked by East Main Box (this signal was used only when 'slipping' coaches from a non-stop train to indicate to drivers that the signals at the other end of the platform were clear); up main 'through' line home signal with, below it, the up main line inner distant for East Main Box; down main relief junction home signal; down main to down main line home signal (this is 'off' for the train) and, below it, the distant signal for West Junction Box (the train is signalled to the Swindon line); down main to down branch (Westbury/Basingstoke) home signal and, below it, the down main to down branch distant signal for Reading Oxford Road Junction box; then lastly the up branch line starting signal to bays 1, 2 or 3, used in conjunction with the mechanical indicator immediately below, and, between the larger arm and the indicator, a small 'calling-on' signal used to allow a loco at caution to enter a platform that is already occupied. In the right foreground is the down bay lines to branch (Westbury/Basingstoke) starting signal; the elevated 'dolly' signal below it is to signal a train into the adjacent sidings.

Left Alas, the manual signalling system has largely vanished. Perhaps this is progress, but a moment's thought on how the system worked shows how breakdowns were very limited in their effect on the system and problems could be isolated quickly and easily - what Hitler's bombers could not do, progress has made possible. The gantry at Reading is no more - featureless colour light signals have replaced it. The box ended its days, as seen here, as the office of a nearby abattoir - what a dreadful indignity!

13.
At the Works

When these pictures were taken in 1960, Doncaster Works - 'The Plant' - was no longer building new steam locomotives but was still actively carrying out heavy repairs. In this process engines were completely taken to pieces and their component parts distributed around the Works to be repaired or replaced. Then everything was re-assembled. Here 'A3' 'Pacific' No 60101 *Cicero* from Haymarket waits outside the Stripping Shop for the beginning of her heavy repair; every part is clearly labelled with her number. 'Pacifics' came in for heavy repair at about 100,000-mile intervals and turnaround time was about 3-4 weeks. This was almost certainly *Cicero*'s last heavy repair before she was withdrawn in April 1963.

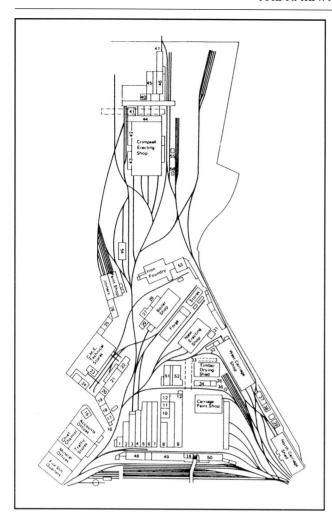

Left Plan of Doncaster Works in the 1950s.

1 Out-station office 2 Rods 3 Machining of cylinders 4 Milling, planing, slotting, etc 5 Turning 6 D shop, brass work 7 Frame bay 8 New machine shop 9 Smiths' shop 10 Machine-fitters' shop 11 White metal 12 Grinding shop 13 Arc welding 14 Coaching control office 15 Library 16 Fire-engine house 17 Inspection office 18 Hydraulic office 19 Electricity office 20 Electric shop 21 Rubber pipe repair 22 Brass foundry 23 Offices 24 Technical stores office 25 Ambulance and first aid room 26 Electric sub-station 27 Flanging shop 28 Boiler shop stores 29 Angle shop 30 Tinsmiths 31 Stores 32 Tyre shed 33 Timber stack 34 Saw mill 35 Timber shed 36 Spray shop 37 Carriage gas shop 38 Stores 39 Tank house 40 Steaming shed 41 Tyre shed 42 Tube house 43 Store 44 Wheel shop 45 Tube repair 46 Engine stripping shop 47 Overhead crane 48 Offices 49 Central drawing office 50 CME's offices 51 Spring shop 52 Plate fabrication 53 Pattern shop 54 Weigh house 55 Air compressors 56 Weigh-bridge

Left Inside the Stripping Shop parts of dismantled engines were every-where. On the right 'K3' No 61974 from Colwick has lost her wheels and it will not be long before her boiler is removed.

Above right Not much is left intact of BR Standard 'Britannia' Class No 70009 *Alfred the Great* from Norwich Thorpe.

Right Overhead travelling cranes were used extensively in railway workshops for lifting and moving heavy parts like this complete boiler.

Left At the time I visited Doncaster its most famous product - No 60103 *Flying Scotsman* - was in for her last heavy repair before her withdrawal and subsequent preservation. Here only *Flying Scotsman*'s main frame and cab remain together.

Right In the boiler shop, boilers were repaired and new ones made. Here riveters work on the top of the boiler of a 'Pacific'; the characteristic 'banjo' dome is clearly seen on the right.

Left It is hard to believe that this shell will shortly become a fully working locomotive boiler. Note the brackets already in place to take the firebox stays.

Above Rivet holes being drilled in a boiler backplate. The operator of the drilling machine has one foot inside what will be the firebox door.

Right Inside the enormous hydraulic press a part is being prepared for pressing. Note the press operator at the controls on the left.

Inside the Wheel Shop at Doncaster there was always an immense assortment of wheels of various shapes and sizes to be seen. The shop was fitted with monorail cranes as can be seen in these pictures. The holes drilled out of the balance weights of the pair of large driving wheels on the extreme right of the upper picture are to do with fine balancing. Note also the squared milled end of the crank pin; this is to take the eccentric which operates the valve gear.

Inside the Forge a coupling rod is being shaped (*above*), then the central grooves are machined out (*right*).

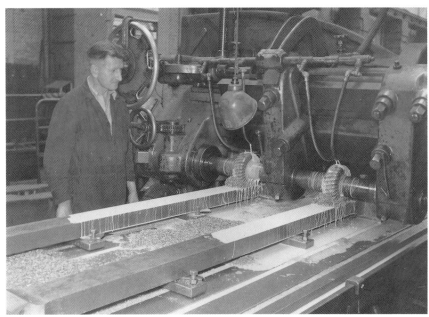

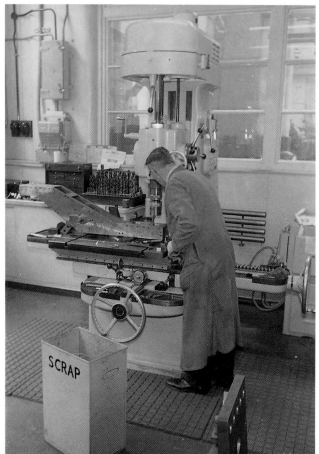

Above In Doncaster's Machine Shop D, the inside cylinder casting of a Thompson three-cylinder locomotive is being set up on one of the boring machines.

Left When meticulously accurate lathe work was required to very fine tolerances, a dust-free air-conditioned workshop was available.

Right In this shot taken in the Iron Foundry, brake blocks are being cast. The weights were used to ensure that the two halves of the mould stayed together during the process.

Below In the Spring Shop a red-hot collar is being tapped on to the centre of a leaf spring, the blades of which are being held together by a special spring vice. When it has cooled, the collar will have shrunk tightly into place.

Left A steel tyre, heated by a circular array of gas jets, is about to be shrunk on to the wheel centre of a pair of wheels belonging to a locomotive pony truck. At Doncaster their bogies always had ten-spoked wheels, whereas at Darlington they were twelve-spoked.

Below In the Crimpsall Erecting Shop Thompson 'B1' 4-6-0 No 61200 is being lifted by the massive overhead travelling crane for moving to another position in the Shop. She was a King's Cross-based locomotive.

Above Now No 61200 is being lowered down on to a temporary 'works bogie' for valve setting. This picture appeared in the October 1960 issue of *Eastern Region Magazine* and the Editor - Ken Mansell - captioned it: 'A symphony in metal with the conductor in the foreground might well be used to describe this action shot at Doncaster Works. A scene perhaps soon to disappear for good.'

Right Doncaster was one the few British locomotive works to have a separate Paint Shop. Here 'B1' Class 4-6-0 No 61182 is being repainted, while behind is 'A2' 'Pacific' No 60530 *Sayajirao*, one of the Peppercorn developments of the Thompson 'A2/2' design.

The Great Western Railway's Swindon Works closed in 1987 and Tarmac Properties took over the site. The town of Swindon had grown up around the Works and no fewer than 15,000 workers were employed there in 1950. The surviving 2,000 were made redundant upon the closure, but Tarmac allowed a few ex-BR employers to operate the former No 20 Shop as Swindon Railway Workshops Ltd and even bought equipment from BR to enable it to service, restore and repair locomotives and stock for private railways - a most worthy cause, one would have thought. More recently, however, Tarmac has terminated this arrangement, and unless there is a change of heart or a rescuer turns up, by the time you read this yet another aspect of the old railway will have vanished for all time. Swindon Railway Workshops, the various small workshops associated with preserved railways and a couple of interesting private ventures were all that remained of the old place where the myriad arts, crafts and skills of the steam railway could survive. Long may that be so.

Left In happier days, visitors to Swindon Works always got the impression of a huge open-plan works with various stages of locomotive building and repair going on all around. In this picture 'Castle' Class 4-6-0 No 5074 *Hampden* is being lifted by one of the overhead cranes.

Below Close by the main frame of 'Hall' Class 4-6-0 No 4983 *Albert Hall*, workers at Swindon discuss aspects of her repair. Note the Automatic Train Control bell still fixed to the side of the locomotive's cab.

Above Another view of the overhaul shop at Swindon Works. There are rows of stripped-down locomotives in the background with boilers removed and only the cab-sides standing. Pistons stand in the foreground with their rods vertical (note the slots at the tip for cotter pins to hold them on the crossheads). Two valves are lying on the ground behind them, just in front of the group of men. These are spindles with a valve head at each end to control admission and exhaust of steam to and from each end of the cylinder - the steam and exhaust rings can be seen shining on each side of the 'bull' ring (spacer).

The front bogie of a 'King' Class 4-6-0 (*below left*), clearly showing the unique 'inside/outside' axleboxes and springing of the leading bogie, and (*below right*) the driven crank axle of a four-cylinder locomotive - note the valve eccentrics in place in the centre.

Left On the Southern Region, Eastleigh Works was also well worth a visit. In this picture a 'Crosti'-boilered 2-10-0 is being repaired behind rebuilt 'Merchant Navy' Class 'Pacific' No 35004 *Cunard White Star*. The latter was a Salisbury-based locomotive, withdrawn in November 1965 and scrapped at Eastleigh in February 1966.

Below Workshops were always places where withdrawn locomotives were scrapped, although such was the scale of withdrawals in the early 'sixties that much work was given out to private contractors. Here at Doncaster '3F' 0-6-0 No 43244 is feeling the bite of the scrapper's torch. These engines were a Johnson Midland Railway design, rebuilt from 1916 onwards by Fowler and fitted with a Belpaire firebox. The Workshops themselves face a very uncertain future. Those remaining are owned by BREL, which itself is now controlled by ASAE Brown Boveri Limited who hold 80 per cent of BREL shares, having recently bought out the Trafalgar House holding. Are the old workshops on the verge of being scrapped too?

14.
On the footplate

Right It was always the dream of every railway enthusiast to ride on the footplate of a main-line express locomotive and, of course, the dream of every small boy once upon a time to become an engine driver. I was indeed privileged, courtesy of Eastern Region's Public Relations Department, to ride on the footplate of *Silver Link* when she hauled the 'Tees-Thames' express out of King's Cross one day in August 1961. The 'Tees-Thames' was a new named express on the ER, appearing first in the timetable in 1960. It departed from King's Cross at 2.00 pm for Saltburn with stops at a number of places including Peterborough, Grantham, York, Doncaster and Middlesbrough.

Silver Link was the original Gresley 'A4' 'Pacific', appearing in September 1935. Here she is at King's Cross about to depart with the 'Tees-Thames'.

Right Immediately after pulling away from King's Cross, you went through the 528-yard Gas Works tunnel, and this is the view from the fireman's side of *Silver Link* on the 1 in 107 rising gradient towards Copenhagen Tunnel. Lying immediately ahead is Belle Isle junction where the branch came in from King's Cross MPD, while the large overbridge carries the North London Line.

Above On the open road, with regulator wide open, *Silver Link* reaches 76 mph with top link King's Cross Driver Oakton in the driver's seat. At that speed the noise level was incredible - one could converse only by shouting directly into the person's ear.

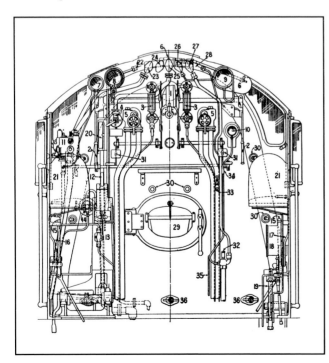

Left Arrangement of footplate fittings of an 'A4' 'Pacific'

1 Regulator stuffing-box 2 Regulator handles 3 Water gauges 4 Blower valve 5 Combined steam and delivery valves 6 Stop valve for steam sand 7 Duplex vacuum gauge 8 Steamchest pressure gauge 9 Boiler pressure gauge 10 Carriage heating pressure gauge 11 Vacuum ejector 12 Reversing screw handle 13 Reversing gear clutch lock 14 Steam sand valve 15 Water control for injectors 16 Sand gear lever 17 Cylinder cock lever 18 Speed recorder 19 Drop-gate screw 20 Cut-off indicator 21 Enginemen's seats 22 Steam sand supply valve 23 Ejector steam stop valve 24 Blank 25 Blower stop valve 26 Pressure gauge stop valve 27 Carriage heating stop valve 28 Mechanical lubricator warming valve 29 Firebox door 30 Washout plugs 31 Remote control for water gauge cocks 32 Carriage heating safety valve 33 Coal watering cock 34 Whistle control 35 Damper rod 36 Handholes

Above Little and often is the rule for efficient firing - too much and the fire bed becomes too thick and valuable gasses are lost in black smoke; too little and steam pressure drops.

Right An essential part of a fireman's duties was to keep the footplate dust-free and he would hose it down from time to time with the steam hose.

Left At Holme we meet and pass the up non-stop 'Elizabethan' headed by one of the regular 'A4s' which worked this prestige service. This time it was No 60009 *Union of South Africa,* one of the 'A4s' privately preserved and which has already been mentioned earlier.

Below The approach to Peterborough. Heading an up express in the platform is one of the brand-new 'Deltics' which were soon to replace the 'Pacifics' on the East Coast routes. They too have now vanished, being replaced by HSTs which themselves are, of course, under threat from the electrics.

Above We coast into the platform at Peterborough with regulator closed. Here we lose *Silver Link* and the train will be worked forward by a New England 'V2'.

Right The 'V2' concerned, No 60867, was not in good shape. Steam was leaking from inside steam pipes and she vibrated so much that I had a hard time to get sharp photographs.

Below right However, under the skilled hands of New England Driver Sid Hankins and his fireman we kept perfect time even if the pictures I got were rather less than ideal.

Above The famous (or infamous) Stoke Bank lay ahead and the following photographs were taken under steadier conditions on another occasion, giving a driver's-eye view from the cab of the prototype 'Deltic' locomotive as Stoke signal box is approached at 75 mph.

Left As the 'Deltic' is about to emerge from Stoke Tunnel, we see an unidentified '01' 2-8-0 struggling up the 1 in 200 gradient with a long freight. Following the successful trails of the prototype 'Deltic', the Eastern Region ordered 22 which were to replace steam on the main expresses of the East Coast route and which became legends in their own right. The 'Deltics' were at the time the most powerful single unit diesel-electric locomotives in the world. English Electric had hoped for overseas orders, and indeed the prototype was fitted with headlamps as used on other railways abroad, but unfortunately no orders materialised and the 22 on the Eastern Region were the only examples ever built. Maybe English Electric priced themselves out of the field or the American diesels were just that much more reliable. We will probably never know.

Above At Grantham on that original occasion I said goodbye to the 'V2' and the 'Tees-Thames' and returned to London in the cab of Brush Type 2 diesel-electric No D5643 heading the up 'Sheffield Pullman'. The quiet comfortable ride in the diesel was an incredible contrast to the noise and dirt of the steam footplate - though far less exciting and exhilarating. One could readily appreciate why many enginemen preferred to drive diesels. With the will, however, cab conditions on steam engines could have been greatly improved as they had been on many US railroads. Here Driver W. Reed of King's Cross has the regulator in the fully open position as the 'Sheffield Pullman' steadily gathers speed on her way to King's Cross.

Right Even though this shot from the cab of a diesel-electric locomotive shows two other diesels, it is a scene which could not be repeated, as the line is now electrified. We are still in the cab of D5643 and about to plunge into Hadley Wood tunnels. Bursting out of the tunnels on the right nearest to us is one of the Pilot Scheme English Electric 'Baby Deltics'; these 1,110 hp diesel-electrics used one Napier 'Deltic' marine engine similar to those used in pairs in the 'Deltics' themselves, but they proved very troublesome in service. On the far right is a Brush Type 2 similar to D5643.

15.
Flying Scotsman

Left Flying Scotsman really must be the most famous steam locomotive of all time. She started out as the third Gresley 'A1' 'Pacific' ordered by the Great Northern railway but emerged from Doncaster in January 1923, immediately after the GNR's grouping into the fledging London & North Eastern Railway. Numbered 4472 under the LNER system, the locomotive was named *Flying Scotsman* after the famous train of the same name and was exhibited, suitably embellished, for two years running in the Hall of Engineering at the British Empire Exhibition at Wembley. In this 1959 photograph, now in BR service with the number 60103, she is pulling out of King's Cross at 5.30 pm with the 'Yorkshire Pullman'.

Below left A few days later and No 60103 *Flying Scotsman* was to be seen in full cry heading the 'Yorkshire Pullman' out of Hadley Wood tunnels but minus headboard. She had been fitted a few months earlier with a double chimney but it was not until 1961 that German-style smoke deflectors were fitted. Other reasons, in the early days, for *Flying Scotsman*'s fame were that, specially fitted with a corridor tender, she was chosen to be one of the two engines which inaugurated the non-stop 'Flying Scotsman' service on 1 May 1928 (the other loco making the simultaneous departure from Edinburgh was No 4476 *Royal Lancer*, later to become BR No 60107); she was the prototype of an extremely popular O-gauge Hornby model; and on 30 November 1934 she was the first Gresley 'Pacific' to reach 100 mph. It is clear that the publicity value of her name influenced LNER authorities in choosing her for the run, knowing that if it was successful there would be immense publicity value for the company.

Above *Flying Scotsman* was a long-time resident at King's Cross MPD where she spent her last years in BR service. In these 1958 pictures Fireman Jack Walsh does the oiling rounds on No 60103 (*left*) and checks the locomotive's brake blocks all round (*right*) shortly before she goes off shed for a spell of duty.

Right Checks and oiling over, Jack puts up the light engine headcode lamp on No 60103's front footplate for the run down to King's Cross. In the background is 'A4' No 60017 *Silver Fox*, with *Silver Link* one of the original four streamlined 'Pacifics' to emerge from Doncaster in 1935 to operate the 'Silver Jubilee' service.

Left Running off towards Belle Isle and then down to King's Cross, this is the driver's eye view from the foot-plate of *Flying Scotsman* as she leaves Top Shed.

Below At King's Cross and now at the head of her train, No 60103 prepares to leave with an easy service that day - the 5.00 pm to Peterborough. She is being driven by Driver Pitman of King's Cross.

Flying Scotsman's withdrawal was accompanied by considerable publicity - here she is about to leave on her very last run for BR, the 1.15 pm to Leeds, and there is an enormous crowd at King's Cross to see her off. *Photo: D. E. Strachan*

Above Now *Flying Scotsman's* second spectacular career was about to start. She had been bought by Alan Peglar and was restored by him at Doncaster to LNER 'A3' livery and fitted with a corridor tender. She was soon hauling specials and during one of the earliest of these she was serviced at Cricklewood Shed, where she is seen being admired by enthusiasts. Alan Peglar, in the centre of the picture, is chatting to Ken Mansell, then Editor of *Eastern Region Magazine*. Ken had been for a number of years Editor of *Railway World* when it was published by Fowlers in Cricklewood and before it was bought by Ian Allan.

Left Alan Peglar poses beside his new acquisition.

Below *Flying Scotsman's* adventures thereafter are too well known to be repeated here. There was the disastrous American trip, the rescue by the Hon W. 'Bill' McAlpine and the triumphant tour of Australia. No 4472 is now back home again delighting everyone who sees her. Perhaps her worksplate bearing the inscription 'London & North Eastern Railway Co, Doncaster, 1923' is a fitting reminder of that great vanishing 'Plant' in the North East which had built No 4472 and had achieved so much.

16.
Lineside

Believe it or not, few railway photographers actually *saw* with the naked eye a steam train going by - they had their eyes glued to their viewfinders and, when steam was supreme, viewfinders were not renowned for giving a good clear life-size image. So even then a railway photographer's main pleasure came from looking at his photographs. Bushey troughs was a favourite location of mine. I lived nearby and in those days a number of nice little bridges spanned the line, over the low parapets of which you could take photographs to your heart's content. Today, what with vandalism and suicide attempts on the electrified main line, those delightful little bridges have been made into impervious tubes - so once again the railway has vanished, if only from sight. In this 1960 picture '4F' 0-6-0 No 44440 works an up slow train of empty freight wagons.

Opposite above From the same location the up 'Caledonian' makes a really fine sight as she picks up water on the troughs. The locomotive is 'Princess Coronation' Class 'Pacific' No 46239 *City of Chester*, one of the originally streamlined engines. Introduced in 1957, the 'Caledonian' was reminiscent of the pre-war 'Coronation Scot'. Leaving Glasgow Central at 8.30 am, the train made only one intermediate stop at Carlisle, with an overall journey time of 6 hr 40 min. Note the Bakerloo Line tube train in the background.

Opposite below The flagship of the West Coast route had been for many years the 'Royal Scot', rivalling the 'Flying Scotsman'. Here the up train is passing Bushey troughs on a rather dull afternoon behind 'Princess Coronation' Class 'Pacific' No 46242 *City of Glasgow*.

Above The 4.30 pm Euston to Liverpool express was named the 'Shamrock' in 1954. Here rebuilt 'Patriot' Class 4-6-0 No 45525 whisks the train past Kings Langley box on a summer's day in 1959.

Left The 'Cambridge Buffet Expresses', or 'Beer Trains' as they were known before the war, were popular services. Here one is seen at Hadley Wood in 1957 hauled by Class 'B1' 4-6-0 No 61139. I recall many a happy journey on this train.

Below An all-time favourite place for railway pictures was the sea wall at Dawlish. Here in the summer of 1959 an unidentified 'King' 4-6-0 runs past with the 'Cornish Riviera Express'. The forerunner of this famous train appeared in July 1904 when the GWR inaugurated a train to Penzance which ran non-stop to Plymouth. July 1906 saw the departure time changed to 10.30 am and the train became known as the 'Cornish Riviera Limited'. The 'Cornish Riviera' name has lived on but there is nothing particularly special about the HST service which now runs between Paddington and Penzance along the route of the old 'Limited'.

Right Living near Woodley in the early 'sixties I had plenty of opportunity to photograph the GW expresses near and in Sonning Cutting. Here is 'King' Class No 6028 *King George VI* heading the down 'Capitals United' in Sonning Cutting. The GWR had a delightful system of train numbering - the actual numbers referred to trains listed in the current Working Timetable, but the letters indicated destinations. 'A' was for London district trains and these could reach as far out Oxford; 'B' was for Bristol trains; 'C' for Cornwall; and 'X' stood for specials. 'F' stood for 'Foreign', ie a service under the Severn into that other country - Wales! The 'Capitals United' was an afternoon express between Paddington and Cardiff.

Below Perhaps my favourite action shot, which for me sums up all the atmosphere of the vanished steam railway, is this 1962 shot taken from the window of Reading West signal box and showing 'Castle' Class 4-6-0 No 5084 *Reading Abbey* with the down 'Wood Lane Milk', a train of empty milk wagons bound for St Erth in Cornwall. This was a regular 'Castle' turn running to Parcels schedules with a speed limit of 45 mph. The return working with full wagons had a 60 mph speed limit and was then known as the 'St Erth Milk'. Here the 'Wood Lane Milk' will shortly vanish into the sunset. Milk, too, has vanished off the railway on to the road. And the steam locomotives have vanished, and with them the glamour which made every one of us once want to be an engine driver.

Index